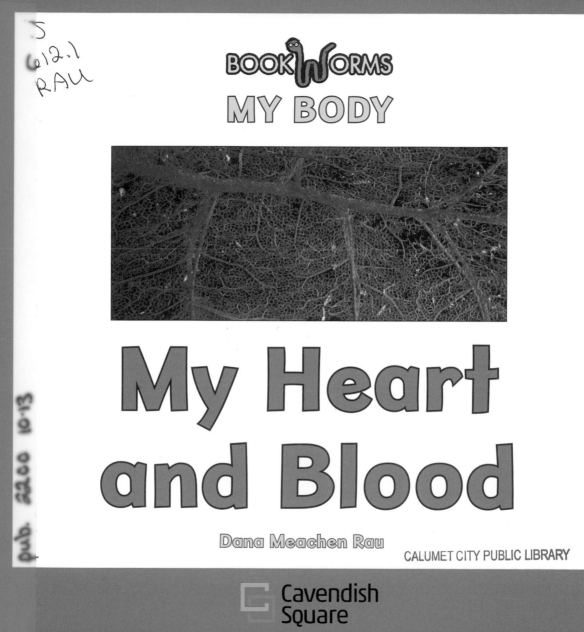

BOOK WORMS

MY BODY

My Heart and Blood

Dana Meachen Rau

Cavendish
Square
New York

Put your hand on your chest. You might be able to feel your heart beating. Your heart is always working. It pumps blood around your body.

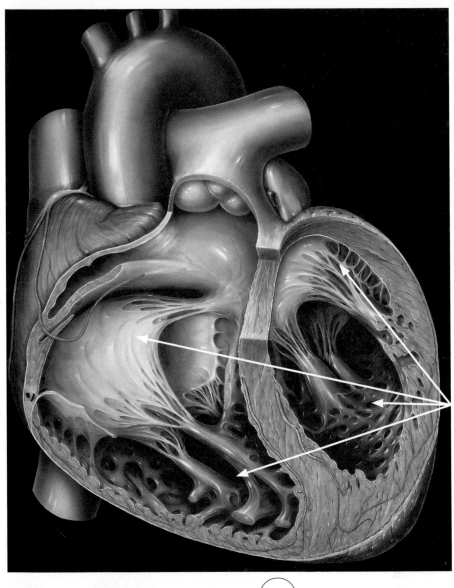

CHAMBERS

Your heart is shaped like a bumpy ball. The rib bones in your chest protect it.

This bumpy ball is hollow inside. It is divided into four parts called **chambers**.

Blood goes into your heart and out again.

The blood travels all over your body. Your heart sends it to your head, your arms and legs, and all your inside parts, too. Then the blood travels back to the heart.

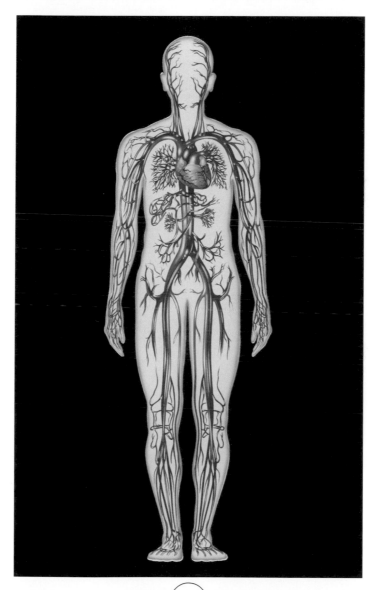

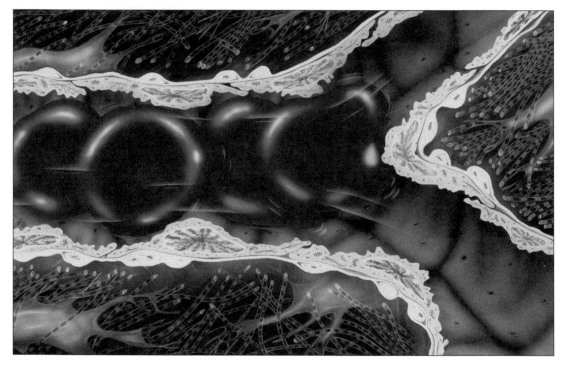

Red blood cells

Your body needs blood because blood is filled with **oxygen**.

Oxygen helps your arms and legs move. It helps you think and breathe.

Red blood cells carry oxygen to all parts of your body.

Blood carries **nutrients** from the food you eat. Your body needs these nutrients to grow.

Blood also collects waste from parts of your body. Waste is material your body cannot use.

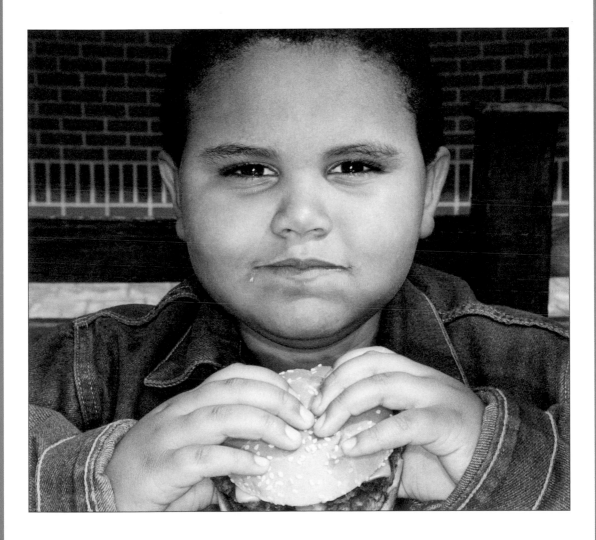

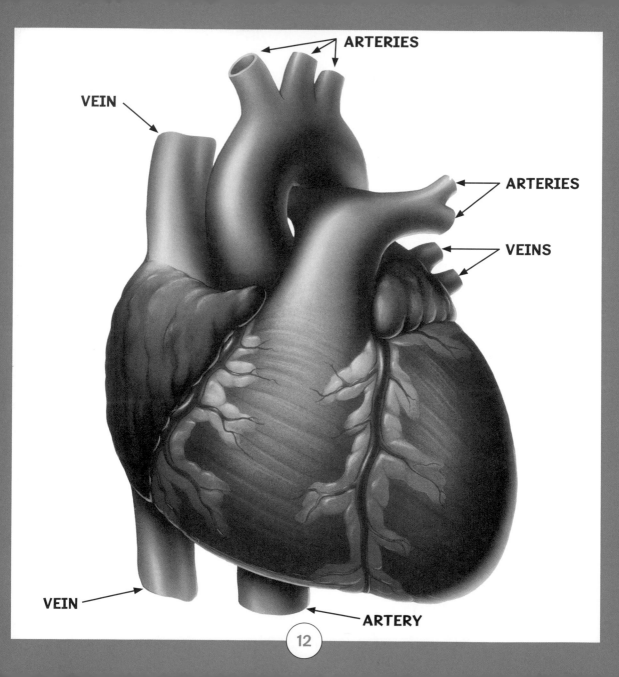

ARTERIES

VEIN

ARTERIES

VEINS

VEIN

ARTERY

Your heart pumps blood to the body through **arteries**. Arteries are tubes that carry blood away from your heart.

Blood goes back to your heart through tubes called **veins**.

Some arteries and veins are very small. They are called **capillaries**.

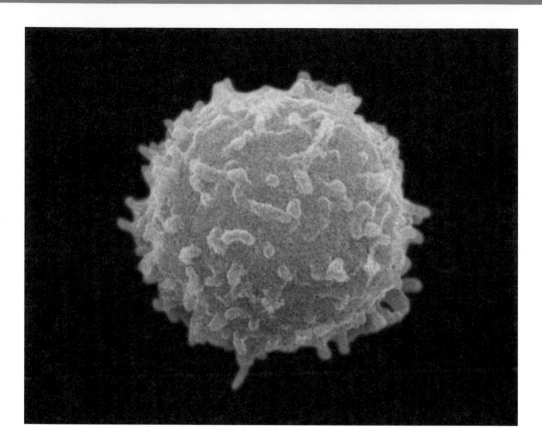

The **white blood cells** in your blood are in charge of protecting your body. They fight **germs**.

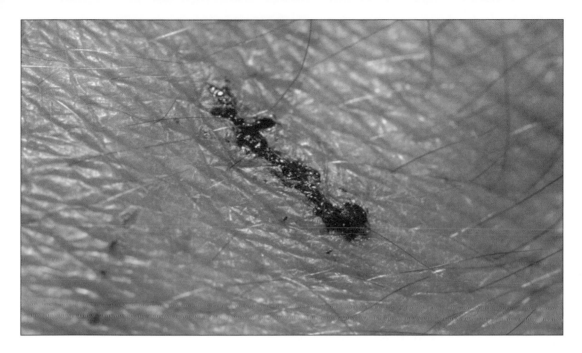

Have you ever cut your finger?
Around your cut, blood gets
thicker and thicker. Then it clots,
or closes, making a scab. Germs
cannot get in.

Your heart, blood, arteries, and veins are called your **circulatory system**.

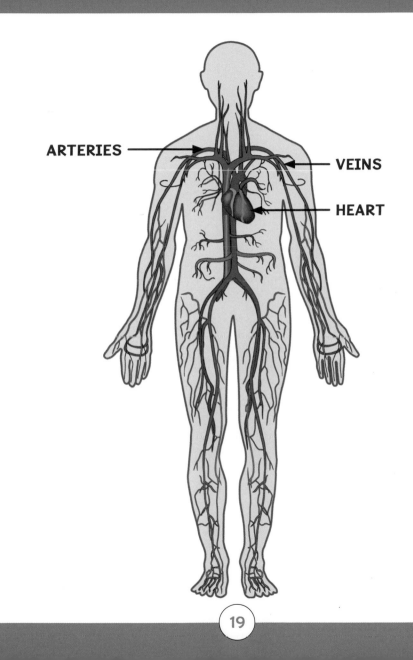

ARTERIES

VEINS

HEART

Sometimes your heart pumps fast. Sometimes it pumps slow. But it is always pumping and keeping you alive.

Challenge Words

arteries (AR-tuh-rees) Tubes that carry blood to all parts of your body.

capillaries (KAP-uh-ler-ees) Very small arteries and veins.

chambers The open spaces inside your heart.

circulatory system (SUR-kyuh-luh-tor-ee SIS-tuhm) Your heart, blood, arteries, and veins.

germs Something that can make you sick.

nutrients (NEW-tree-uhnts) The parts of food your body needs to stay healthy.

oxygen (OK-si-juhn) The part of air your body needs to work.

red blood cells The part of the blood that carries oxygen.

veins Tubes that carry blood to your heart.

white blood cells The part of the blood that fights germs.

Index

With thanks to Nanci Vargus, Ed. D. and Beth Walker Gambro, reading consultants

Published in 2014 by Cavendish Square Publishing, LLC
303 Park Avenue South, Suite 1247, New York, NY 10010

Website: cavendishsq.com

This publication represents the opinions and views of the author based on his or her personal experience, knowledge, and research. The information in this book serves as a general guide only. The author and publisher have used their best efforts in preparing this book and disclaim liability rising directly or indirectly from the use and application of this book.

CPSIA Compliance Information: Batch #WS13CSQ

All websites were available and accurate when this book was sent to press.

Library of Congress
Cataloging-in-Publication Data

Rau, Dana Meachen, 1971–
My heart and blood / Dana Meachen Rau.
— 2nd ed.
p. cm. — (Bookworms: my body)
Includes index.
Summary: "Gives young readers an introduction to the importance and function of the heart and blood in the body"—Provided by publisher.
ISBN 978-1-60870-434-7 (hardcover)
ISBN 978-1-62712-034-0 (paperback)
ISBN 978-1-62712-002-9 (ebook)
1. Cardiovascular system—Juvenile literature.
I. Title.
QP103.R38 2013
612.1—dc23   2012002623

Editor: Christina Gardeski
Art Director: Anahid Hamparian
Series Designer: Virginia Pope

Photo research by Bethany Larson

Cover: © moodboard / Alamy
Title Page: *Photo Researchers, Inc.*, Biophoto Association

The photographs in this book are used by permission and through courtesy of: *Corbis*: Pat Doyle, p. 11; Jim Cummins, p. 20; Royalty Free, p. 3. *Custom Medical Stock Photo*: p. 17. *Cavendish Square Publishing, LLC*: p. 19. *Photo Researchers, Inc.*: Brian Evans, p. 12; Medical Art Service, p. 4; John Bavosi, p. 7; Michel Gilles, p. 8; Biophoto Association, p. 15. *Visuals Unlimited*: Dr. Donald Fawcett and E. Shelton, p. 16.

Printed in the United States of America